LEVEL 1 HASKINS

Haskins, Lori.

Busy tractors, busy days

A Note to Parents

DK READERS is a compelling program for beginning readers, designed in conjunction with leading literacy experts, including Dr. Linda Gambrell, Professor of Education at Clemson University. Dr. Gambrell has served as President of the National Reading Conference, the College Reading Association, and the International Reading Association.

Beautiful illustrations and superb full-color photographs combine with engaging, easy-to-read stories to offer a fresh approach to each subject in the series. Each DK READER is guaranteed to capture a child's interest while developing his or her reading skills, general knowledge, and love of reading.

The five levels of DK READERS are aimed at different reading abilities, enabling you to choose the books that are exactly right for your child:

Pre-level 1: Learning to read
Level 1: Beginning to read
Level 2: Beginning to read alone
Level 3: Reading alone
Level 4: Proficient readers

The "normal" age at which a child begins to read can be anywhere from three to eight years old. Adult participation through the lower levels is very helpful for providing encouragement, discussing storylines, and sounding out unfamiliar words.

No matter which level you select, you can be sure that you are helping your child learn to read, then read to learn!

DK

LONDON, NEW YORK, MUNICH,
MELBOURNE, AND DELHI

U.S. Editor Nancy Ellwood
Assistant Editor Liza Kaplan
Managing Art Editor Michelle Baxter

Designer Marc J. Cohen

Reading Consultant
Linda Gambrell, Ph.D.

First Edition, 2010
10 11 12 13 14 10 9 8 7 6 5 4 3 2 1
Published in the United States by DK Publishing
375 Hudson Street, New York, New York 10014

Created and produced by
Parachute Publishing, L.L.C.
322 Eighth Avenue
New York, New York 10001

DK books are available at special discounts when purchased in bulk
for sales promotions, premiums, fund-raising, or educational use.
For details, contact:
DK Publishing Special Markets
375 Hudson Street
New York, New York 10014
SpecialSales@dk.com

A catalog record for this book is available
from the Library of Congress.

ISBN: 978-0-7566-4454-3 (Paperback)
ISBN: 978-0-7566-4453-6 (Hardcover)

Printed in China
First printing January 2010

The publisher would like to thank the following for their kind
permission to reproduce their photographs:

ABBREVIATIONS KEY:
t-top, b-bottom, r-right, l-left, c-center, a-above, f-far,
bkgd-background

8-9 iwka/Shutterstock.com (8bfl);
Elena Schweitzer/Shutterstock.com (8bc, 8br, 9bfl, 9bcl, 9bcr, 9bfr);
10-11 hans.slegers/Shutterstock.com (10bfl); Andrjuss/
Shutterstock.com (10bc, 10br, 11bfl, 11bcl, 11bc); a9photo/
Shutterstock.com (11bcr); Rgbspace/Dreamstime.com (11bfr)
12-13 Nancy Hochmuth/Shutterstock.com (12bfl); Scott Karcich/
Shutterstock.com (12bc); Dole/Shutterstock.com (12br);
Igor Dutina/Shutterstock.com (13bcl); Elena Schweitzer/
Shutterstock.com (13bcr); Joe Gough/Shutterstock.com (13bcr);
Tomboy2290/Dreamstime.com (13bfr)
14-15 PeppPic/Shutterstock.com (14bc); Jostein Hauge/
Shutterstock.com (14br); Kitzman/Shutterstock.com (15bfl);

latentlight/Shutterstock.com (15bcl); Kostenko Max
Shutterstock.com (15bcr); Lorna/Dreamstime.com (15
16-17 Heather Prosch-Jensen/Shutterstock.com (16b
KennStilger47/Shutterstock.com (16br); Robert Kyl
Shutterstock.com (17bcl); Nancy Gill/Shutterstock.com
Charlene Bayerle/Shutterstock.com (17bcr); 18-19 Merri
Shutterstock.com (18bfl); Jody Dingle/Shutterstock.com
juan carlos tinjaca/Shutterstock.com (18br); dcwcreat
Shutterstock.com (19bl); Dennis Donohue/Shutterstock
(19bc); dcwcreations/Shutterstock.com (19br)
20-21 Anobis/Shutterstock.com (20bfl); elena moisee
Shutterstock.com (20bc, 20br, 21bfl, 21bcl, 21bcr); Jarno C
Zarraonandia/Shutterstock.com (21bfr)
22-23 fengzheng/Shutterstock.com (22bfl); Nancy Bran
Shutterstock.com (22bc); slowfish/Shutterstock.com (2
Kuzma/Shutterstock.com (23bl); Greenfire/Shutterstock
(23bc); Shi Yali/Shutterstock.com (23br)
24-25 tacojim/iStockphoto.com (24bfl); zeremski/iStockph
(24bc); El Greco/Shutterstock.com (24br); Northswed
Shutterstock.com (25bl); Joel Blit/Shutterstock.com (2
nycshooter/iStockphoto.com (25br)
26-27 Oleg – F/Shutterstock.com (26bfl); David Reil
Shutterstock.com (26bc); Rob Byron/Shutterstock.com (
Henry William Fu/Shutterstock.com (27bl); yui/Shutterstc
(27bc); nikkytok/Shutterstock.com (27br)
29 Jim Parkin/Shutterstock.com (bfl); Nancy Hixson/Shut
com (bcl) 32 Bg_knight/Dreamstime.com (lac)

All other images © Deere & Company.

Every effort has been made to trace the copyright holde
photographs, and we apologize if any omissions have been

Discover more at
www.dk.com

DK READERS

LEARNING
pre-level **1**
TO READ

JOHN DEERE

Busy Tractors, Busy Days

Written by Lori Haskins Houran

DK Publishing

PARACHUTE PRESS

Tractors are busy
machines. They work
hard every day.

This busy tractor plows the field.

plows

field

plow

This busy tractor plants the seeds.

seeds

rrow

planter

This busy tractor weeds the crops.

crops

blade

combine

corn

corn

This busy tractor helps
to harvest the corn.

spout

baler

hay

 bales

This busy tractor bales the hay.

bale fork

bale

barns

This busy tractor brings the hay bale to the barn.

This busy tractor pulls
the wagon.

 wagons

wagon

mixe

cows

feed

feed

This busy tractor delivers the animal feed.

This busy tractor cuts the grass in the pasture. There are lots of fences to work around.

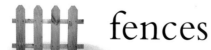 fences

pasture

mower

23

This busy tractor plows the snow.

road

snow blower

snow

snow

This busy tractor dumps the gravel.

 gravel

loader bucket

Today this busy tractor
gets a tune-up.
Then it's back to work!

safety light

engin

  tires

plowing

planting

Which job do you like best?

dumping

baling

Glossary

Bale
a bundle of dry hay

Crop
a plant grown in
a farmer's field

Furrow
a long, narrow cut
dug by a plow

Plow
a tool that digs
rows in a field

Tractor
a vehicle that does
many jobs on and
off the farm